Writings: from the inside

W. A. James

Writings: From The Inside
Copyright © 2018 by Art James

All rights reserved. No part of this publication may be reproduced, distributed, or transmitted in any form or by any means, including photocopying, recording, or other electronic or mechanical methods, without the prior written permission of the author, except in the case of brief quotations embodied in critical reviews and certain other non-commercial uses permitted by copyright law.

Tellwell Talent
www.tellwell.ca

ISBN
978-0-2288-0260-0 (Hardcover)
978-0-2288-0258-7 (Paperback)
978-0-2288-0259-4 (eBook)

CONTENTS

Dedication...i
Acknowledgement iii
Foreword...v
My Heart 1
Intimacy 2
My Love 3
Gracefull / Awkward 4
Time 5
Life's Ladder 6
Mother Light 7
To Be... 8
Seeking 9
Trust.. 10
Entitlement 11
Blaming.. 12
Dissatisfied 13
True Form 14
Being Knowing 15
Trouble 16
Beauty... 17

Alone	18
Loss	19
Friendship	20
Solid Ground	21
Labels	22
Liquid Knowing	23
Childlike	24
Broken Shell	25
The Creators Playground	26
The Storm Of Love	27
In Closing	28

DEDICATION

To my wife Audrey

We are apart ...
Yet bound together by a bond ...
Not of this reality...
but of a dimension where
there is only love and compassion ...
The ties ...
That bond of being ...
Allows us the wisdom to be who we are ..
Follow separate paths ...
Love forever ...

Arthur

ACKNOWLEDGEMENT

My children, Caroline, David, Patrick and Michael.
Your love and support has carried me through
Some difficult times.
I will be grateful to you all forever.
To my good friend Susan Kolenz
Who, is not only a friend
But, who prepared this manuscript for print,
Discerning my handwriting without complaint.

Love you all.

FOREWORD

These writings are not meant to teach...
They are meant to touch ...
To touch that space in you where you already know who you are...

If you are still and quiet in that space it will grow to where you realize,
the beauty and magnitude of you ....

From there you can share that space with all you encounter...

Allowing you to shed light to others and "in that" you continually allow You to expand to that space ...

You are fully ... You

P.S. I am not there yet, but I am moving forward to that space.

MY HEART

If you take my heart ..
Don't take it with hardened clutching hands..
That want to reshape it .. mould it ..
Into what you perceive it should be ..
Change the beat to match your own..
So that you are not lonely ..
Then return it .. It will not fit..
Atrophies and dies ...
If you take my heart
Take it with softened hands ...
Caress it gently ...
Hold it close to you so I may
Know your heart beat ...
I know you ...
Then when you return it..
Which you must..
It will fit perfectly into
the cavity of my soul ..

INTIMACY

It is the bird song
Given freely without
Desire for reward..

It is the garden
And its emotion
The water to flourish..

It is the tree
That shades from the
Never ending heat of this reality..

It is the nourishment
When no mortal food could
Pass your lips..

It is the fire
That warms the very
Core of you being..

It is the peace
From pain that is
Unbearable and endless..

And in the end
The wings that bear
You up to the source
To that absolute, where
There is only love..

MY LOVE

You are heavy for me to bear
Your beingness...
The soft caress ...
Gentle touch ...
The warmth of your body.

So hard to accept ...
Can I love enough to be worthy ...
Or shall I simply allow the gift of You..
To overcome the obstacles in loving.

GRACEFULL / AWKWARD

Graceful ... A\wkward ...
They are the same ..
Watch the seagull, flying ..
Soaring .. playing with the wind..
Being its purpose .. Graceful...
It lands .. Walking ..
Concrete .. Grass .. Awkward ..
But still being its purpose ..
Like us .. in grace .. aware.. we fly
Soar, playing with being...graceful
We land,..
Walking.. in relationships.. patterns..
In Love... In life ... Awkward ...
But still beingness.. knowing ..
We gather awareness inside ...
Again ... Flying.. soaring ... Beautiful life ...
Delicate in meaning ... Our place to fly ...
Always

TIME

Wasted .. Wanted ..
Desired to relive ..
We have only now ..
This is the time.
This moment.
The only Value ...
Are you living?
Do you exist?
In this now
Only you exist ...
Mind time, wasted ...
Heart time ... wanted ..
Now time .. this moment
You .. real ..
Aware of this now time ..
How precious ..
What value this moment ...
All of you .. vast, knowing ..
Loving in now time ..

LIFE'S LADDER

At the breast, warm, loved,
Heart beat to heart beat..
I am .. growing, wanting, needing.
Recognize patterns .. they are effective,
A new person emerging ...
Recognizing me .. That person known ..
Expanding patterns give
Feelings of security ..
What is missing .. Something ..
I must be more .. Unsure..
Restless .. Safe in patterns ..
The familiar, built by me for me..
Who am I...
Older, unsure – afraid.
Must be more .. knowing more..
Nearing death – AH! At the breast ..
Peaceful, heart beat to eternal
Heart beat, going .. knowing ..
Loving at last.

MOTHER LIGHT

Mother light to all..
To those you co-created...
Know you are mother light ..
A purpose .. a way of being ..
Intended .. Part of the deep silence ...
You mother love your being ..
Mother light.. from there ..
To space that can see ..
To space that is blind with patterns.. dissolving ..
Softly .. gently .. bright ..

Mother light

TO BE

To be who .. who ..
What is known well?
Who all around me knows
Know yourself .. be yourself..
The writer says..
Know greater than yourself
The teacher says..
Born in the image and likeness ...
Of who.. of what ..
I don't know the image ..
Can't see the likeness ..
How to be what is not known..
Search, inside .. outside..
Searching a path shaped
Like a circle .. no end ...
Be still – turmoil all around ..
No quiet space .. make space
Between thoughts .. " So Many"
Yet be still .. somewhere ..
Known .. Is that where to be is ..
So small ... magnificent, such
Magnitude .. to be this ..
Longing to be all that is.

SEEKING

We seek from each other ..
A book .. a poem .. a teacher .. a lover..
Always looking outside ..
Open Gently the door to your heart ..
Walk slowly in .. space .. peace..
Be in awe of your inner knowing ..
It is yours not a gift .. a part of you ..
Who you are .. believe it .. love it ..
It will guide you to truth .. love,
Wholeness ... ONENESS ...
To You who you seek.

TRUST

Trust .. and I receive life's
Greatest gift ..
I am vulnerable ...
There I can love unconditionally ..
Trust .. shattered ..
By a single word or deed ..
Designed to siege my vulnerability ..
My desire to love ..
Shattered .. but be still .. vulnerable ..
I can love ...
Protect ... build a wall around me ...
Hide my heart and knowing ...
The love is lost ...
The shattered heart is pain ..
From this I learn ..
In sorrow if I fail ..
In loving if I can accept the pain ..
Taking me to places of love yet unknown..
Trusted ... beautiful .. as we are ...

ENTITLEMENT

The good I do ... The love I express
The enlightenment I may acquire
All are gifts ...
When I am entitled,
I miss the joy of gracious receiving..
I miss the warmth of the giver..

I am not entitled to anything.

Entitlement hardens my heart...
Builds wall around what I know
Shuts out the opinions and paths of others.

It leave me separated and lonely.

BLAMING

Blaming is my barrier, to protect my heart..
To cover my vulnerability, I am right you are wrong.

The way not to blame, to tear down this barrier.
Is to act, move, speak, from a heart that is open ... compassionate
In this I cannot blame because in softness and compassion I find the real me ...

DISSATISFIED

If I am dissatisfied with you.

I must only become
completely and compassionately satisfied with me...

Then my dissatisfaction has no meaning, no value in true relationships.

TRUE FORM

In true form we are like the trees..

Delicate, fragile leaves, firmly grounded.

Constant growth.

Accepting of change and our inevitable return to that from which

we came.

BEING KNOWING

On the spiritual journey.
I begin to truly know, a little at first..
the space of it will grow in stillness.
This is good,
But until I BE what I know..
I am merely a droning drumbeat from afar.

TROUBLE

Why this trouble … it is a gift for me, a blessing.
So that I can compassionately see myself,
and what I must learn in it.

When I can achieve this in trouble.
I can express that compassion to all who are part of it.

Then we all move from a place of softened heart.
The only space from which we should act.

BEAUTY

The true beauty of a tree
Is underground, unseen.
What I see is only the manifestation in form..
Of the miracle below.

Underground lies roots to the source,
nourishment, stability, strength and growth.

I am the same, in stillness I go deeper into my underground.
There I find my unseen, that miracle of my true beauty,
once seen I can manifest it thru me in form.

ALONE

In life .. in Love .. in Death ..

ALONE

Never lonely .. alone.. how wondrous
The stillness of alone ..
That which gives all I require …
Alone .. to see .. to know.. to be ..
The magnificence of who I am …
I the creator … comes when I am
Still .. Alone .. I see my beauty ..
Power .. compassion .. it is good ..
I am alone.

LOSS

The Great Gift..

Accumulate all ...
It matters not how generous or caring I have been,
that is how I should be.

The gift is not the things, or the sharing,
the gift is losing it all before I pass.

This provides the path of clarity,
So that the journey to the next is carefree,
fearless, and to be desired.
PREPARE FOR PASSING

Heal all wounds
Remove all chaos
Express compassion
Know who you are
Create peace all around you
Examine in stillness
Embrace the newness of absolute love
That awaits you
At the moment of
The end of this part of your journey.

FRIENDSHIP

So difficult ..
Compromise to satisfy ..
Change for approval,
Need, ego, love, alone
All trying to fit .. reality ..
Melting together, but
Travelling separate paths ..
To the same end..
Not my way .. not your way ..
The way .. with space to be different ..
Time to hold that space ..
My time .. Your time..
Me in your space..
You in my space ..
to each a trust ..
Emotion, not thrust ..
Desire controlled ...
Strong .. loving .. friends

SOLID GROUND

In stillness ..
In the space between thoughts
I will always find solid ground.

The learned teacher can take me,
To that space ...
But be aware ... that space is filled
With the essence of the teacher ...
I can never become the essence
Of another ... I can only
Be the essence of me ...

Be that .. you will find your
Solid ground there ....

LABELS

I starve in this life.
Unable to find that
Which will nourish and restore ...
Give real meaning ...

In this hunger
I open the doors to where
My heart is stored ...
Where all real nourishment abides.

I look gently not at my heart
It is pure ...
Look gently again at what ...
Labeled containers, neat,
Tidy, prepared and labeled by me!
Which do I choose ... ego ... pain ...
Hate ... greed ... lust... worry ... anger... love...
Each will ease my hunger for a while..
They are comfort .. security .. identity for today..
I know them all intimately ...
I choose the one unlabelled ...
If I am open to consume, to allow..
To be ok with its texture and taste
It will provide all the newness,
Nourishment to sustain and grow ..
I will dissolve all that is labelled...
It contains what which my heart has prepared...
With love, kindness and true compassion.
If I can consume it all ...
I am satisfied ...
I am real ...

LIQUID KNOWING

Knowing … a beautiful space to be in ..
The danger of knowing, is that I know firmly!
From this I build walls around it,
Protect it, shield the vulnerability
Of me in it and my fear of not knowing …
That level of knowing closes me off from the knowing of those who know different from me …
Then I am unable to see different knowing and therefore unable to touch the being of those different from what I know
Because of my fear of being challenged…
My knowing is my security and I will not have it questioned …
The price of this is separation …
Separation from one is separation from all..
In that what value is there in firm knowing.

Knowing is not a destination, rather a resting place to prepare for the never ending journey ahead.

When knowing is liquid, it flows from openness to all hearts.

CHILDLIKE

A child .. newborn .. aged
Always a child .. simple..
Trusting .. loving .. open..
A mind uncluttered ...
A pure heart ..
Consciousness not immersed in thought ..
A glow of authenticity ..
A reflection of reality ..
Mindless of life or death ..
Simply being .. wanting ..
To be childlike .. forever..

BROKEN SHELL

In a shell I live..
From a shell I give.
Yearning for the broken yoke.
I know beyond my shelled enclosure..
Fear of breaking.
That which encases.. comforts..
Protects.. yet longing for
Free.. the pain..
Vulnerability looms dark
With light encrusted newness.
Shining who I am to me
And beyond.
Glowing in the shadow of the anticipated breaking...
Is failing, the end of this you...
The climax of this me... NO!
Only the inch movement
Forward, deeper, to the knowing..
To outward expression of real...
Through feeble forms..

THE CREATORS PLAYGROUND

The beingness of intimacy is the playground of love.

I swing until I am over the bar ...

Fearless, vulnerable, joyful, one with the swing...

As if I could fly ... I can..
Straining to go higher... faster...
Not wanting to end.

The merry go round spins until I am dizzy with love...
And I am one with all..
one with the act of loving and spinning.

Skipping as if my feet were grounded in air..

The thrill of the touch ...
Giving all of me to the moment ...
To joy.. to the swing ... letting it take me where it will.

Intimacy is the creators playground but I must move the swing...
Giving all of me, being willing to fall...
Trusting me and the swing ...
Then I let go and the creator takes me home...

THE STORM OF LOVE

Flesh given freely,
Open, warm to the touch,
Soft and yielding, yet.
Burning with desire and need..
Not needing for the flesh alone..
But needing for oneness ...
A joining, not lust or passion ...
But of that beautiful blend
Of desire and spirit.. Of beingness ...
Being one with
Simple beingness, moulded
Together with that one true
Being of creation ... the power
Of surrender joined by oneness ...
Slow, growing, touching, talking ...
Playing.. the storm gathering
From a gentle breeze to
The uprooting of withholding..
The shelter from its own storm..
The eye gentle while all around
The emotion and spirit are swirling...
THE BOLT!
Then spent, the gentle breeze
Again is blowing, fresh with
Rain of the storm, soothing
To the uprooting of even that
Which was hidden and secured ..
Allowing eyes to see anew.

IN CLOSING

I write, hopefully, from inside of me...
Allowing something greater than me to guide my pen.

Allow yourself to soften ...
Hold out your open hands and your heart will be the pen to write your way.
Compassionately yours,

W. A. James

www.ingramcontent.com/pod-product-compliance
Lightning Source LLC
LaVergne TN
LVHW011901060526
838200LV00054B/4456